T0354583

PONGO'S WORLD
AND HiS FAMiLY

Katheryn Skalet

Balboa Press books may be ordered through booksellers or by contacting:

Balboa Press
A Division of Hay House
1663 Liberty Drive
Bloomington, IN 47403
www.balboapress.com
844-682-1282

ISBN: 979-8-7652-5460-8 (sc)
ISBN: 979-8-7652-5461-5 (hc)
ISBN: 979-8-7652-5459-2 (e)

Library of Congress Control Number: 2024916706

Print information available on the last page.

Balboa Press rev. date: 08/09/2024

BALBOA.PRESS
A DIVISION OF HAY HOUSE

PONGO'S WORLD
AND HiS FAMiLY

Pongo and Family

My Great Dane and I love to play

We can play fetch, I hide treats for him, and he loves to run around.

I love to bake for my Pongo!! He loves biscuits and ice cubes!

Pongo and I can go to the beach, explore the sand, and the water.

We can go on an easy hike, too steep of a terrain will hurt their hips, legs and shoulders! I never want my Pongo to be in pain. I never want anything bad to happen to him!

Pongo and Jeff go to the vet
to make sure he is okay!

The vet gives him plenty of treats
to distract Pongo while the
veterinarian looks him over.

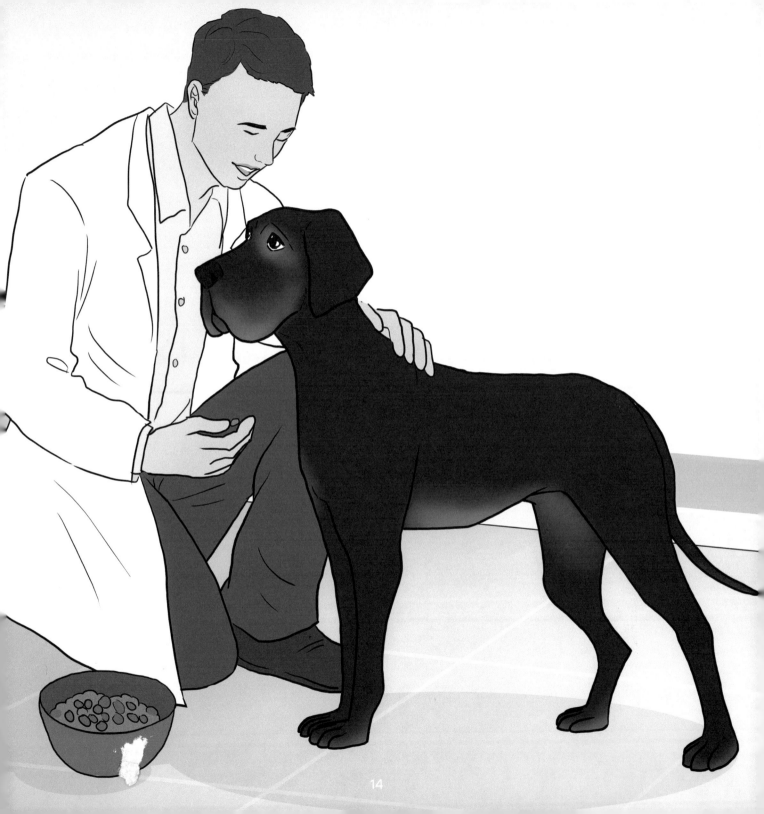

I always give him some leftovers. I always wonder does he even chew them? That's why I always have to be careful of what I allow him to chew on for the toys sake!

He is too big for dog costumes, so we usually put Pongo in Jeff's clothing.

Pongo is silly, he's goofy, he reminds me of Goofy from the Mickey Mouse cartoons but he's unique like a snowflake and as heavy as a pony.

Pongo likes to jump on my bed with me and we nap together.

After surgery he would be my cane and help me stand up. He is always at my side after the my stay at the hospital. We would do relaxing things like watching a movie together.

My Great Dane and I are best friends. Nothing will ever change that. Even if he steals hamburgers off the counter. Which is a pretty easy feat for him being that he's just as tall as the countertops!

What would I do without Pongo he is the reason I feel safe at night. He may be too big for a slide but he'll jump in the pool!

Pongo main job is my protector. He knows exactly how to warn off bad guys. He can bark so loud all the neighbors can hear.

At the end of the day I know I have Pongos back and he knows that we have his.